Blessing the Boats

New and Selected Poems 1988–2000

by

LUCILLE CLIFTON

BOA Editions, Ltd. ■ Rochester, NY ■ 2000

LC #: 00–131741

ISBN: 1–880238–88–8 paper

00 01 02 03   7 6 5 4 3

Publications by BOA Editions, Ltd.—
a not-for-profit corporation under section 501 (c) (3)
of the United States Internal Revenue Code—
are made possible with the assistance of grants from
the Literature Program of the New York State Council on the Arts,
the Literature Program of the National Endowment for the Arts,
the Lannan Foundation, the Sonia Raiziss Giop Charitable Foundation,
the Eric Mathieu King Fund of The Academy of American Poets,
The Halcyon Hill Foundation, as well as from
the Mary S. Mulligan Charitable Trust, the County of Monroe, NY,
Towers Perrin, and the Estate of EMK

*   *   *

See page 132 for special individual acknowledgments.

Cover Design: Geri McCormick
Typesetting: Richard Foerster
Manufacturing: McNaughton & Gunn, Lithographers
BOA Logo: Mirko

NYSCA

BOA Editions, Ltd.
Steven Huff, Publisher
Richard Garth, Chair, Board of Directors
A. Poulin, Jr., President & Founder (1976–1996)
260 East Avenue
Rochester, NY 14604

www.boaeditions.org

for Russell
1963–1997

the beautiful boy
has entered
the beautiful city

contents

from *The Terrible Stories* (1996)

new poems
(2000)

the times

it is hard to remain human on a day
when birds perch weeping
in the trees and the squirrel eyes
do not look away but the dog ones do
in pity.
another child has killed a child
and i catch myself relieved that they are
white and i might understand except
that i am tired of understanding.
if this
alphabet could speak its own tongue
it would be all symbol surely;
the cat would hunch across the long table
and that would mean time is catching up,
and the spindle fish would run to ground
and that would mean the end is coming
and the grains of dust would gather themselves
along the streets and spell out:

these too are your children   this too is your child

■

signs

when the birds begin to walk
when the crows in their silk tuxedos
stand in the road and watch
as oncoming traffic swerves to avoid
the valley of dead things
when the geese reject the sky
and sit on the apron of highway 95
one wing pointing north the other south

and what does it mean this morning
when a man runs wild eyed from his car
shirtless and shoeless his palms spread wide
into the jungle of traffic into a world
gone awry the birds beginning to walk
the man almost naked almost cawing
almost lifting straining to fly

■

moonchild

whatever slid into my mother's room that
late june night, tapping her great belly,
summoned me out roundheaded and unsmiling.
is this the moon, my father used to grin,
cradling me?   it was the moon
but nobody knew it then.

the moon understands dark places.
the moon has secrets of her own.
she holds what light she can.

we girls were ten years old and giggling
in our hand-me-downs. we wanted breasts,
pretended that we had them, tissued
our undershirts. jay johnson is teaching
me to french kiss, ella bragged, who
is teaching you? how do you say; my father?

the moon is queen of everything.
she rules the oceans, rivers, rain.
when I am asked whose tears these are
I always blame the moon.

■

dialysis

after the cancer, the kidneys
refused to continue.
they closed their thousand eyes.

blood fountains from the blind man's
arm and decorates the tile today.
somebody mops it up.

the woman who is over ninety
cries for her mother.   if our dead
were here they would save us.

we are not supposed to hate
the dialysis unit.   we are not
supposed to hate the universe.

this is not supposed to happen to me.
after the cancer the body refused
to lose any more.   even the poisons
were claimed and kept

until they threatened to destroy
the heart they loved.   in my dream
a house is burning.

something crawls out of the fire
cleansed and purified.
in my dream i call it light.

after the cancer i was so grateful
to be alive.   i am alive and furious.
Blessed be even this?

■

donor

to lex

when they tell me that my body
might reject
i think of thirty years ago
and the hangers i shoved inside
hard trying to not have you.

i think of the pills, the everything
i gathered against your
inconvenient bulge; and you
my stubborn baby child,
hunched there in the dark
refusing my refusal.

suppose my body does say no
to yours.   again, again i feel you
buckled in despite me, lex,
fastened to life like the frown
on an angel's brow.

■

libation

north carolina, 1999

i offer to this ground,
this gin.
i imagine an old man
crying here
out of the overseer's sight,

pushing his tongue
through where a tooth
would be if he were whole.
the space aches
where his tooth would be,

where his land would be, his
house   his wife   his son
his beautiful daughter.

he wipes his sorrow from
his cheek, then
puts his thirsty finger
to his thirsty tongue
and licks the salt.

i call a name that
could be his.
this offering
is for you old man;
this salty ground,
this gin.

■

the photograph: a lynching

is it the cut glass
of their eyes
looking up toward
the new gnarled branch
of the black man
hanging from a tree?

is it the white milk pleated
collar of the woman
smiling toward the camera,
her fingers loose around
a christian cross drooping
against her breast?

is it all of us
captured by history into an
accurate album? will we be
required to view it together
under a gathering sky?

■

jasper   texas   1998

for j. byrd

i am a man's head hunched in the road.
i was chosen to speak by the members
of my body.   the arm as it pulled away
pointed toward me, the hand opened once
and was gone.

why and why and why
should i call a white man brother?
who is the human in this place,
the thing that is dragged or the dragger?
what does my daughter say?

the sun is a blister overhead.
if i were alive i could not bear it.
the townsfolk sing we shall overcome
while hope bleeds slowly from my mouth
into the dirt that covers us all.
i am done with this dust.   i am done.

■

alabama 9/15/63

Have you heard the one about
the shivering lives,
the never to be borne daughters and sons,

the one about Cynthia and Carole and Denise and Addie Mae?
Have you heard the one about
the four little birds
shattered into skylarks in the white
light of Birmingham?

Have you heard how the skylarks,
known for their music,
swooped into heaven, how the sunday
morning strains shook the piano, how the blast
is still too bright to hear them play?

■

what i think when i ride the train

maybe my father
made these couplers.
his hands were hard
and black and swollen,
the knuckles like lugs
or bolts in a rich man's box.
he broke a bone each year
as if on schedule.
when i read about a wreck,
how the cars buckle
together or hang from the track
in a chain, but never separate,
i think; see,
there's my father,
he was a chipper,
he made the best damn couplers
in the whole white world.

■

praise song

to my aunt blanche
who rolled from grass to driveway
into the street one sunday morning.
i was ten.   i had never seen
a human woman hurl her basketball
of a body into the traffic of the world.
Praise to the drivers who stopped in time.
Praise to the faith with which she rose
after some moments then slowly walked
sighing back to her family.
Praise to the arms which understood
little or nothing of what it meant
but welcomed her in without judgment,
accepting it all like children might,
like God.

■

august

for laine

what would we give,
my sister,
to roll our weak
and foolish brother

back onto his bed,
to face him with his sins
and blame him
for them?

what would we give
to fuss with him again,
he who clasped his hands
as if in prayer and melted

to our mother?   what
would we give
to smile and staple him
back into our arms,

our honey boy, our sam,
not clean, not sober, not
better than he was, but
oh, at least, alive?

■

study the masters

like my aunt timmie.
it was her iron,
or one like hers,
that smoothed the sheets
the master poet slept on.
home or hotel, what matters is
he lay himself down on her handiwork
and dreamed.   she dreamed too, words:
some cherokee, some masai and some
huge and particular as hope.
if you had heard her
chanting as she ironed
you would understand form and line
and discipline and order and
america.

∎

lazarus

first day

i rose from stiffening
into a pin of light
and a voice calling
"Lazarus, this way"
and i floated or rather
swam in a river of sound
toward what seemed to be
forever   i was almost
almost there when i heard
behind me
"Lazarus, come forth" and
i found myself twisting
in the light for this
is the miracle, mary martha;
at my head and at my feet
singing my name
was the same voice

■

lazarus

second day

i am not the same man
borne into the crypt.

as ones return from otherwhere
altered by what they have seen,

so have i been forever.
lazarus.
lazarus who was dead.

what entered the light was one man.
what walked out is another.

■

lazarus

third day

on the third day i contemplate
what i was moving from
what i was moving toward

light again and
i could hear the seeds
turning in the grass   mary
martha i could feel the world

now i sit here in a crevice
on this rock   stared at
answering questions

sisters stand away
from the door to my grave
the only truth i know

■

birthday 1999

it is late.   the train
that is coming is
closer.   a woman can hear it
in her fingers, in her knees,
in the space where her uterus
was.   the platform feels
filled with people
but she sees no one else.
she can almost hear the
bright train eye.
she can almost touch the cracked
seat labeled lucille.
someone should be with her.
someone should undress her
stroke her one more time
and the train
keeps coming closer.

it is a dream i am having
more and more and more.

■

grief

begin with the pain
of the grass
that bore the weight
of adam,
his broken rib mending
into eve,

imagine
the original bleeding,
adam moaning
and the lamentation of grass.

from that garden,
through fields of lost
and found, to now, to here,
to grief for the upright
animal, to grief for the
horizontal world.

pause then for the human
animal in its coat
of many colors.   pause
for the myth of america.
pause for the myth
of america.

and pause for the girl
with twelve fingers
who never learned to cry enough
for anything that mattered,

not enough for the fear,
not enough for the loss,
not enough for the history,
not enough

for the disregarded planet.
not enough for the grass.

then end in the garden of regret
with time's bell tolling grief
and pain,
grief for the grass
that is older than adam,
grief for what is born human,
grief for what is not.

■

report from the angel of eden

i found them there
rubbing against the leaves
so that the nubs of their
wings were flush under their skin

and it seemed like dancing
as when we angels
praise among the clouds
but they were not praising You

i watched
the grass grow soft and rich
under their luminous bodies
and their halos begin to fade

it was like dancing
creation flowered around them
moaning with delight   they were
trembling and i knew

a world was being born
i feared for their immortality
i feared for mine
under the strain of such desire

i knew
they could do evil
with it and i knew
they would

when i remembered what i was
i swiveled back unto Your grace
still winged i think but wondering
what now becomes   what now

of Paradise

■

from *next*
(1988)

album

for lucille chan hall

1   it is 1939.
    our mothers are turning our hair
    around rags.
    our mothers
    have filled our shirley temple cups.
    we drink it all.

2   1939 again.
    our shirley temple curls.
    shirley yellow.
    shirley black.
    our colors are fading.

later we had to learn ourselves
back across 2 oceans
into bound feet and nappy hair.

3   1958 and 9.
    we have dropped daughters,
    afrikan and chinese.
    we think
    they will be beautiful.
    we think
    they will become themselves.

4   it is 1985.
    she is.
    she is.
    they are.

■

why some people be mad at me sometimes

they ask me to remember
but they want me to remember
their memories
and i keep on remembering
mine

■

sorrow song

for the eyes of the children,
the last to melt,
the last to vaporize,
for the lingering
eyes of the children, staring,
the eyes of the children of
buchenwald,
of viet nam and johannesburg,
for the eyes of the children
of nagasaki,
for the eyes of the children
of middle passage,
for cherokee eyes, ethiopian eyes,
russian eyes, american eyes,
for all that remains of the children,
their eyes,
staring at us,   amazed to see
the extraordinary evil in
ordinary men.

■

female

there is an amazon in us.
she is the secret we do not
have to learn.
the strength that opens us
beyond ourselves.
birth is our birthright.
we smile our mysterious smile.

■

my dream about being white

hey music and
me
only white,
hair a flutter of
fall leaves
circling my perfect
line of a nose,
no lips,
no behind, hey
white me
and i'm wearing
white history
but there's no future
in those clothes
so I take them off and
wake up
dancing.

■

my dream about the cows

and then I see the cattle of my own town,
rustled already,
prodded by pale cowboys with a foreign smell
into dark pens built to hold them forever,
and then I see a few of them
ribs thin and weeping low over
sparse fields and milkless lives but
standing somehow standing,
and then I see how all despair is
thin and weak and personal and
then I see it's only
the dream about the cows.

■

my dream about time

a woman unlike myself is running
down the long hall of a lifeless house
with too many windows which open on
a world she has no language for,
running and running until she reaches
at last the one and only door
which she pulls open to find each wall
is faced with clocks and as she watches
all of the clocks strike
                        NO

■

my dream about falling

a fruitful woman
such as myself
is
falling
notices
she is
an apple
thought
that the blossom
was always
thought
that the tree
was forever
fruitful
a woman
such as
myself.

                        the fact is the falling.
                        the dream is the tree.

■

my dream about the second coming

mary is an old woman without shoes.
she doesn't believe it.
not when her belly starts to bubble
and leave the print of a finger where
no man touches.
not when the snow in her hair melts away.
not when the stranger she used to wait for
appears dressed in lights at her
kitchen table.
she is an old woman and
doesn't believe it.

when Something drops onto her toes one night
she calls it a fox
but she feeds it.

■

my dream about God

He is wearing my grandfather's hat.
He is taller than my last uncle.
when He sits to listen
He leans forward tilting the chair

where His chin cups in my father's hand.
it is swollen and hard from creation.
His fingers drum on His knee
dads stern tattoo.

and who do i dream i am
accepting His attentions?

i am the good daughter who stays at home
singing and sewing.
when i whisper He strains to hear me and
He does whatever i say.

■

my dream about the poet

a man.
i think it is a man.
sits down with wood.
i think he's holding wood.
he carves.
he is making a world
he says
as his fingers cut citizens
trees and things
which he perceives to be a world
but someone says that is
only a poem.
he laughs.
i think he is laughing.

■

the death of thelma sayles

2/13/59
age 44

i leave no tracks so my live loves
can't follow. at the river
most turn back, their souls shivering,
but my little girl stands alone on the bank
and watches. i pull my heart out of my pocket
and throw it. i smile as she catches all
she'll ever catch and heads for home
and her children. mothering
has made it strong, i whisper in her ear
along the leaves.

■

lives

to lu in answer to her question

you have been a fisherman,
simple and poor. you
struggled all your days and
even at the end you fought
and did not win. your son
was swimming. fearing
for his life you
rushed toward him. and drowned.

once a doctor, bitter,
born in a cold climate,
you turned your scalpel
on the world and cut your way
to the hangman.

humans who speak of royal lives
amuse Them. you have heard of course
of the splendid court of sheba;
you were then. you were not there.

■

the message of thelma sayles

baby, my only husband turned away.
for twenty years my door was open.
nobody ever came.

the first fit broke my bed.
i woke from ecstasy to ask
what blood is this? am i the bride of Christ?
my bitten tongue was swollen for three days.

i thrashed and rolled from fit to death.
you are my only daughter.

when you lie awake in the evenings
counting your birthdays
turn the blood that clots on your tongue
into poems. poems.

■

the death of fred clifton

11/10/84
age 49

i seemed to be drawn
to the center of myself
leaving the edges of me
in the hands of my wife
and i saw with the most amazing
clarity
so that i had not eyes but
sight,
and, rising and turning,
through my skin,
there was all around not the
shapes of things
but oh, at last, the things
themselves.

■

shapeshifter poems

1

the legend is whispered
in the women's tent
how the moon when she rises
full
follows some men into themselves
and change them there
the season is short
but dreadful   shapeshifters
they wear strange hands
they walk through the houses
at night   their daughters
do not know them

2

who is there to protect her
from the hands of the father
not the windows which see and
say nothing   not the moon
that awful eye   not the woman
she will become with her
scarred tongue   who   who   who   the owl
laments into the evening   who
will protect her   this   prettylittlegirl

3

if the little girl lies
still enough
shut enough
hard enough
shapeshifter may not
walk tonight
the full moon may not
find him here
the hair on him
bristling
rising
up

4

the poem at the end of the world
is the poem the little girl breathes
into her pillow   the one
she cannot tell   the one
there is no one to hear   this poem
is a political poem   is a war poem   is a
universal poem but is not about
these things   this poem
is about one human heart   this poem
is the poem at the end of the world

■

from *quilting*
(1991)

quilting

somewhere in the unknown world
a yellow eyed woman
sits with her daughter
quilting.

some other where
alchemists mumble over pots.
their chemistry stirs
into science. their science
freezes into stone.

in the unknown world
the woman
threading together her need
and her needle
nods toward the smiling girl
remember
this will keep us warm.

how does this poem end?
      do the daughters' daughters quilt?
      do the alchemists practice their tables?
      do the worlds continue spinning
      away from each other forever?

■

white lady

a street name for cocaine

wants my son
wants my niece
wants josie's daughter
holds them hard
and close as slavery
what will it cost
to keep our children
what will it cost
to buy them back.

white lady
says i want you
whispers
let me be your lover
whispers
run me through your
fingers
feel me smell me taste me
love me
nobody understands you like
white lady

white lady
you have chained our sons
in the basement
of the big house
white lady
you have walked our daughters
out into the streets
white lady
what do we have to pay

to repossess our children
white lady
what do we have to owe
to own our own at last

■

the birth of language

and adam rose
fearful in the garden
without words
for the grass
his fingers plucked
without a tongue
to name the taste
shimmering in his mouth
did they draw blood
the blades   did it become
his early lunge
toward language
did his astonishment
surround him
did he shudder
did he whisper
eve

■

sleeping beauty

when she woke up
she was terrible.
under his mouth her mouth
turned red and warm
then almost crimson as the coals
smothered and forgotten
in the grate.
she had been gone so long.
there was much to unlearn.
she opened her eyes.
he was the first thing she saw
and she blamed him.

■

poem in praise of menstruation

if there is a river
more beautiful than this
bright as the blood
red edge of the moon   if

there is a river
more faithful than this
returning each month
to the same delta   if there

is a river
braver than this
coming and coming in a surge
of passion, of pain   if there is

a river
more ancient than this
daughter of eve
mother of cain and of abel   if there is in

the universe such a river   if
there is some where water
more powerful than this wild
water
pray that is flows also
through animals
beautiful and faithful and ancient
and female and brave

■

peeping tom

sometimes at night he dreams back
thirty years
to the alley outside our room
where he stands, a tiptoed boy,
watching the marvelous thing,
a man turning into a woman.
sometimes
beating himself with his own fist
into that spilled boy and the
imagined world of that man
that woman that night, he lies
turned from his natural wife.
sometimes he searches the window for
a plaid cap, two wide eyes.

■

wild blessings

licked in the palm of my hand
by an uninvited woman. so i have held
in that hand the hand of a man who
emptied into his daughter, the hand
of a girl who threw herself
from a tenement window, the trembling
junkie hand of a priest, of a boy who
shattered across viet nam
someone resembling his mother,
and more. and more.
do not ask me to thank the tongue
that circled my fingers
or pride myself on the attentions
of the holy lost.
i am grateful for many blessings
but the gift of understanding,
the wild one, maybe not.

■

photograph

my grandsons
spinning in their joy

universe
keep them turning   turning
black blurs against the window
of the world
for they are beautiful
and there is trouble coming
round and round and round

■

lot's wife   1988

each of these weeds is a day
i climbed the stair
at 254 purdy street
and looked into a mirror
to see if i was really there
i was there.   i am there.
in the thousand days.
the weeds.   and these weeds

were 11 harwood place
that daddy bought expecting it
to hold our name forever
against the spin of the world.

our name is spinning away in the wind
blowing across the vacant lots
of buffalo, new york,
that were my girlhood homes.

sayles, i hear them calling, sayles,
we thought we would live forever;
and i look back like lot's wife
wedded to her weeds and turn to something
surer than salt and write this, yes
i promise, yes we will.

■

poem to my uterus

you   uterus
you have been patient
as a sock
while i have slippered into you
my dead and living children
now
they want to cut you out
stocking i will not need
where i am going
where am i going
old girl
without you
uterus
my bloody print
my estrogen kitchen
my black bag of desire
where can i go
barefoot
without you
where can you go
without me

■

to my last period

well girl, goodbye,
after thirty-eight years.
thirty-eight years and you
never arrived
splendid in your red dress
without trouble for me
somewhere, somehow.

now it is done,
and i feel just like
the grandmothers who,
after the hussy has gone,
sit holding her photograph
and sighing, *wasn't she
beautiful? wasn't she beautiful?*

■

wishes for sons

i wish them cramps.
i wish them a strange town
and the last tampon.
i wish them no 7-11.

i wish them one week early
and wearing a white skirt.
i wish them one week late.

later i wish them hot flashes
and clots like you
wouldn't believe.   let the
flashes come when they
meet someone special.
let the clots come
when they want to.

let them think they have accepted
arrogance in the universe,
then bring them to gynecologists
not unlike themselves.

∎

How art thou fallen from Heaven
O Lucifer, son of the morning? . . .
—Isaiah 14:12

oh where have you fallen to
son of the morning
beautiful lucifer
bringer of light
it is all shadow
in heaven without you
the cherubim sing
kaddish

    and even the
solitary brother
has risen from his seat
of stones   he is holding
they say   a wooden stick
and pointing toward
a garden

    light breaks
where no light was before
where no eye is prepared
to see
and animals rise up to walk
oh lucifer
what have you done

■

remembering the birth of lucifer

some will remember
the flash of light
as he broke
from the littlest finger
of God   some will
recall the bright shimmer
and then
flush in the tremble of air
so much shine

even then   the seraphim say
they knew
it was too much for
one small heaven
they rustled their three wings
they say   and began
to wait   and to watch

■

whispered to lucifer

lucifer six-finger
where have you gone to
with your swift lightning

oh son of the morning
was it the woman
enticed you to leave us

was it to touch her
featherless arm
was it to curl your belly

around her
that you fell laughing
your grace all ashard

leaving us here in
perpetual evening
even the guardians

silent   all of us
going about our
father's business

less radiant
less sure

■

eve's version

smooth talker
slides into my dreams
and fills them with apple
apple snug as my breast
in the palm of my hand
apple sleek apple sweet
and bright in my mouth

it is your own lush self
you hunger for
he whispers   lucifer
honey-tongue.

■

lucifer understanding at last

thy servant lord

bearer of lightning
and of lust

thrust between the
legs of the earth
into this garden

phallus and father
doing holy work

oh sweet delight
oh eden

if the angels
hear of this

there will be no peace
in heaven

■

the garden of delight

for some
it is stone
bare smooth
as a buttock
rounding
into the crevasse
of the world

for some
it is extravagant
water   mouths wide
washing together
forever   for some
it is fire
for some air

and for some
certain only of the syllables
it is the element they
search their lives for

eden

for them
it is a test

■

adam thinking

she
stolen from my bone
is it any wonder
i hunger to tunnel back
inside   desperate
to reconnect the rib and clay
and to be whole again

some need is in me
struggling to roar through my
mouth into a name
this creation is so fierce
i would rather have been born

■

eve thinking

it is wild country here
brothers and sisters coupling
claw and wing
groping one another

i wait
while the clay two-foot
rumbles in his chest
searching for language to

call me
but he is slow
tonight as he sleeps
i will whisper into his mouth
our names

■

the story thus far

so they went out
clay and morning star
following the bright back
of the woman

as she walked past
the cherubim
turning their fiery swords
past the winged gate

into the unborn world
chaos fell away
before her like a cloud
and everywhere seemed light

seemed glorious
seemed very eden

■

lucifer speaks in his own voice

sure as i am
of the seraphim
folding wing
so am i certain of a
graceful bed
and a soft caress
along my long belly
at endtime   it was
to be
i who was called son
if only of the morning
saw that some must
walk or all will crawl
so slithered into earth
and seized the serpent in
the animals   i became
the lord of snake for
adam and for eve
i   the only lucifer
light-bringer
created out of fire
illuminate i could
and so
illuminate i did

■

blessing the boats

(at St. Mary's)

may the tide
that is entering even now
the lip of our understanding
carry you out
beyond the face of fear
may you kiss
the wind then turn from it
certain that it will
love your back   may you
open your eyes to water
water waving forever
and may you in your innocence
sail through this to that

■

from *the book of light*
(1993)

imagining bear

for alonzo moore sr.

imagine him too tall and too wide
for the entrance into parlors

imagine his hide gruff, the hair on him
grizzled even to his own hand

imagine his odor surrounding him,
rank and bittersweet as bark

imagine him lumbering as he moves
imagine his growl filling the wind

give him an old guitar
give him a bottle of booze

imagine his children laughing; papa   papa
imagine his wife sighing; oh lonnie

imagine him singing, imagine his granddaughter
remembering him in poems

■

the women you are accustomed to

wearing that same black dress,
their bronzed hair set in perfect place,
their lips and asses tight;
these women gathered in my dream
to talk their usual talk,
their conversation spiked with the names
of avenues in France.

and when i asked them what the hell,
they shook their marble heads
and walked erect out of my sleep,
back into a town which knows
all there is to know
about the cold outside, while i relaxed
and thought of you,
your burning blood, your dancing tongue.

■

song at midnight

> . . . do not
> send me out
> among strangers
> —Sonia Sanchez

brothers,
this big woman
carries much sweetness
in the folds of her flesh.
her hair
is white with wonderful.
she is
rounder than the moon
and far more faithful.
brothers,
who will hold her,
who will find her beautiful
if you do not?

■

here yet be dragons

so many languages have fallen
off of the edge of the world
into the dragon's mouth. some

where there be monsters whose teeth
are sharp and sparkle with lost

people. lost poems. who
among us can imagine ourselves
unimagined? who

among us can speak with so fragile
tongue and remain proud?

■

the yeti poet returns to his village to tell his story

. . . found myself wondering
if i had entered
the valley of shadow

found myself wandering
a shrunken world
of hairless men

oh the pouches
they close themselves into
at night   oh the thin
paps of their women

i turned from the click
of their sprit-catching box
the boom of their long stick

and made my way back
to this wilderness
where we know where we are
what we are

■

crabbing

(the poet crab speaks)

pulling
into their pots
our wives
our hapless children.
crabbing
they smile, meaning us
i imagine,
though our name
is our best secret.
this forward moving
fingered thing
inedible
even to itself,
how can it understand
the sweet sacred meat
of others?

■

the earth is a living thing

is a black shambling bear
ruffling its wild back and tossing
mountains into the sea

is a black hawk circling
the burying ground circling the bones
picked clean and discarded

is a fish black blind in the belly of water
is a diamond blind in the black belly of coal

is a black and living thing
is a favorite child
of the universe
feel her rolling her hand
in its kinky hair
feel her brushing it clean

■

if i should

to clark kent

enter the darkest room
in my house and speak
with my own voice, at last,
about its awful furniture,
pulling apart the covering
over the dusty bodies; the randy
father, the husband holding ice
in his hand like a blessing,
the mother bleeding into herself
and the small imploding girl,
i say if i should walk into
that web, who will come flying
after me, leaping tall buildings?
you?

■

further note to clark

do you know how hard this is for me?
do you know what you're asking?

what i can promise to be is water,
water plain and direct as Niagara.
unsparing of myself, unsparing of
the cliff i batter, but also unsparing
of you, tourist. the question for me is
how long can i cling to this edge?
the question for you is
what have you ever traveled toward
more than your own safety?

■

final note to clark

they had it wrong,
the old comics.
you are only clark kent
after all. oh,
mild mannered mister,
why did i think you could fix it?
how you must have wondered
to see me taking chances,
dancing on the edge of words,
pointing out the bad guys,
dreaming your x-ray vision
could see the beauty in me.
what did i expect? what
did i hope for? we are who we are,
two faithful readers,
not wonder woman and not superman.

■

note, passed to superman

sweet jesus, superman,
if i had seen you
dressed in your blue suit
i would have known you.
maybe that choirboy clark
can stand around
listening to stories
but not you, not with
metropolis to save
and every crook in town
filthy with kryptonite.
lord, man of steel,
i understand the cape,
the leggings, the whole
ball of wax.
you can trust me,
there is no planet stranger
than the one i'm from.

■

leda 1

there is nothing luminous
about this.
they took my children.
i live alone in the backside
of the village.
my mother moved
to another town. my father
follows me around the well,
his thick lips slavering,
and at night my dreams are full
of the cursing of me
fucking god fucking me.

■

leda 2

a note on visitations

sometimes another star chooses.
the ones coming in from the east
are dagger-fingered men,
princes of no known kingdom.
the animals are raised up in their stalls
battering the stable door.
sometimes it all goes badly;
the inn is strewn with feathers,
the old husband suspicious,
and the fur between her thighs
is the only shining thing.

■

leda 3

a personal note (re: visitations)

always pyrotechnics;
stars spinning into phalluses
of light, serpents promising
sweetness, their forked tongues
thick and erect, patriarchs of bird
exposing themselves in the air.
this skin is sick with loneliness.
You want what a man wants,
next time come as a man
or don't come.

■

far memory

a poem in seven parts

1
convent

my knees recall the pockets
worn into the stone floor,
my hands, tracing against the wall
their original name, remember
the cold brush of brick, and the smell
of the brick powdery and wet
and the light finding its way in
through the high bars.

and also the sisters singing
at matins, their sweet music
the voice of the universe at peace
and the candles their light the light
at the beginning of creation
and the wonderful simplicity of prayer
smooth along the wooden beads
and certainly attended.

2

someone inside me remembers

that my knees must be hidden away
that my hair must be shorn
so that vanity will not test me
that my fingers are places of prayer
and are holy   that my body is promised
to something more certain
than myself

3
again

born in the year of war
on the day of perpetual help.

come from the house
of stillness
through the soft gate
of a silent mother.

come to a betraying father.
come to a husband who would one day
rise and enter a holy house.

come to wrestle with you again,
passion, old disobedient friend,
through the secular days and nights
of another life.

4
trying to understand this life

who did i fail, who
did i cease to protect
that i should wake each morning
facing the cold north?

perhaps there is a cart
somewhere in history
of children crying "sister
save us" as she walks away.

the woman walks into my dreams
dragging her old habit.
i turn from her, shivering,
to begin another afternoon
of rescue, rescue.

5
sinnerman

horizontal one evening
on the cold stone,
my cross burning into
my breast, did i dream
through my veil
of his fingers digging
and is this the dream
again, him, collarless
over me, calling me back
to the stones of this world
and my own whispered
hosanna?

6
karma

the habit is heavy.
you feel its weight
pulling around your ankles
for a hundred years.

the broken vows
hang against your breasts,
each bead a word
that beats you.

even now
to hear the words
defend
protect
goodbye
lost or
alone
is to be washed in sorrow.

and in this life
there is no retreat
no sanctuary
no whole abiding
sister.

7
gloria mundi

so knowing,
what is known?
that we carry our baggage
in our cupped hands
when we burst through
the waters of our mother.
that some are born
and some are brought
to the glory of this world.
that it is more difficult
than faith
to serve only one calling
one commitment
one devotion
in one life.

■

from *The Terrible Stories*
(1996)

telling our stories

the fox came every evening to my door
asking for nothing. my fear
trapped me inside, hoping to dismiss her
but she sat till morning, waiting.

at dawn we would, each of us,
rise from our haunches, look through the glass
then walk away.

did she gather her village around her
and sing of the hairless moon face,
the trembling snout, the ignorant eyes?

child, i tell you now it was not
the animal blood i was hiding from,
it was the poet in her, the poet and
the terrible stories she could tell.

■

fox

. . . The foxes are hungry, who could blame them
for what they do? . . .
                    —"Foxes in Winter"
                    Mary Oliver

who
can blame her for hunkering
into the doorwells at night,
the only blaze in the dark
the brush of her hopeful tail,
the only starlight
her little bared teeth?

and when she is not satisfied
who can blame her for refusing to leave,
for raising the one paw up and barking,
Master Of The Hunt, why am i
not feeding, not being fed?

■

the coming of fox

one evening i return
to a red fox
haunched by my door.

i am afraid
although she knows
no enemy comes here.

next night again
then next then next
she sits in her safe shadow

silent as my skin bleeds
into long bright flags
of fur.

■

dear fox

it is not my habit
to squat in the hungry desert
fingering stones, begging them
to heal, not me but the dry mornings
and bitter nights.
it is not your habit
to watch. none of this
is ours, sister fox.
tell yourself that anytime now
we will rise and walk away
from somebody else's life.
any time.

■

leaving fox

so many fuckless days and nights.
only the solitary fox
watching my window light
barks her compassion.
i move away from her eyes,
from the pitying brush
of her tail
to a new place and check
for signs. so far
i am the only animal.
i will keep the door unlocked
until something human comes.

■

one year later

what if,
then,
entering my room,
brushing against the shadows,
lapping them into rust,
her soft paw extended,
she had called me out?
what if,
then,
i had reared up baying,
and followed her off
into vixen country?
what then of the moon,
the room, the bed, the poetry
of regret?

■

a dream of foxes

in the dream of foxes
there is a field
and a procession of women
clean as good children
no hollow in the world
surrounded by dogs
no fur clumped bloody
on the ground
only a lovely line
of honest women stepping
without fear or guilt or shame
safe through the generous fields

■

amazons

when the rookery of women
warriors all
each cupping one hand around
her remaining breast

daughters of dahomey
their name fierce on the planet

when they came to ask
who knows what you might have
to sacrifice   poet   amazon
there is no choice

then when they each
with one nipple lifted
beckoned to me
five generations removed

i rose
and ran to the telephone
to hear
    cancer   early detection   no
    mastectomy   not yet

there was nothing to say
my sisters swooped in a circle dance
audre was with them and i
had already written this poem

■

lumpectomy eve

all night i dream of lips
that nursed and nursed
and the lonely nipple

lost in loss and the need
to feed that turns at last
on itself   that will kill

its body for its hunger's sake
all night i hear the whispering
the soft

        love calls you to this knife
        for love   for love

all night it is the one breast
comforting the other

        ∎

1994

i was leaving my fifty-eighth year
when a thumb of ice
stamped itself near my heart

you have your own story
you know about the fear the tears
the scar of disbelief

you know the saddest lies
are the ones we tell ourselves
you know how dangerous it is

to be born with breasts
you know how dangerous it is
to wear dark skin

i was leaving my fifty-eighth year
when i woke into the winter
of a cold and mortal body

thin icicles hanging off
the one mad nipple weeping

have we not been good children
did we not inherit the earth

but you must know all about this
from your own shivering life

■

hag riding

why
is what i ask myself
maybe it is the afrikan in me
still trying to get home
after all these years
but when i wake to the heat of morning
galloping down the highway of my life
something hopeful rises in me
rises and runs me out into the road
and i lob my fierce thigh high
over the rump of the day and honey
i ride   i ride

■

rust

we don't like rust,
it reminds us that we are dying.
—Brett Singer

are you saying that iron understands
time is another name for God?

that the rain-licked pot is holy?
that the pan abandoned in the house

is holy? are you saying that they
are sanctified now, our girlhood skillets

tarnishing in the kitchen?
are you saying we only want to remember

the heft of our mothers' handles,
their ebony patience, their shine?

∎

slaveships

loaded like spoons
into the belly of Jesus
where we lay for weeks for months
in the sweat and stink
of our own breathing
Jesus
why do you not protect us
chained to the heart of the Angel
where the prayers we never tell
and hot and red
as our bloody ankles
Jesus
Angel
can these be men
who vomit us out from ships
called Jesus   Angel   Grace Of God
onto a heathen country
Jesus
Angel
ever again
can this tongue speak
can these bones walk
Grace Of God
can this sin live

■

memphis

. . . *at the river i stand,*
guide my feet, hold my hand

i was raised
on the shore
of lake erie
e is for escape

there are more s'es
in mississippi
than my mother had
sons

this river never knew
the kingdom of dahomey

the first s
begins in slavery
and ends in y
on the bluffs

of memphis
why are you here
the river wonders
northern born

looking across from buffalo
you look into canada toronto
is the name of the lights
burning at night

the bottom of memphis
drops into the nightmare
of a little girl's fear
in fifteen minutes

they could be here
i could be there
mississippi
not the river   the state

schwerner
and chaney
and goodman

medgar

schwerner
and chaney
and goodman
and medgar

my mother had one son
he died gently near lake erie

some rivers flow back
toward the beginning
i never learned to swim

will i float or drown
in this memphis
on the mississippi river

what is this southland
what has this to do with egypt
or dahomey
or with me

so many questions
northern born

■

memory

ask me to tell how it feels
remembering your mother's face
turned to water under the white words
of the man at the shoe store. ask me,
though she tells it better than i do,
not because of her charm
but because it never happened
she says,
no bully salesman swaggering,
no rage, no shame, none of it
ever happened.
i only remember buying you
your first grown up shoes
she smiles. ask me
how it feels.

■

what did she know, when did she know it

in the evenings
what it was the soft tap tap
into the room   the cold curve
of the sheet arced off
the fingers sliding in
and the hard clench against the wall
before and after
all the cold air   cold edges
why the little girl never smiled
they are supposed to know everything
our mothers   what did she know
when did she know it

■

lorena

it lay in my palm soft and trembled
as a new bird and i thought about
authority and how it always insisted
on itself, how it was master
of the man, how it measured him, never
was ignored or denied and how it promised
there would be sweetness if it was obeyed
just like the saints do, like the angels,
and i opened the window and held out my
uncupped hand. i swear to god,
i thought it could fly

■

heaven

my brother is crouched at the edge
looking down.
he has gathered a circle of cloudy
friends around him
and they are watching the world.

i can feel them there, i always could.
i used to try to explain to him
the afterlife,
and he would laugh. he is laughing now,

pointing toward me. "she was my sister,"
i feel him say,
"even when she was right, she was wrong."

■

acknowledgments

Grateful acknowledgment is made to Copper Canyon Press for permission to reprint poems from *the book of light*, Copyright © 1993 by Lucille Clifton.

Two lines from *House of Light* by Mary Oliver. Copyright © 1990 by Mary Oliver. Reprinted by permission of Beacon Press, Boston.

■

about the author

Lucille Clifton is the author of ten books of poetry and seventeen books for children. Her honors include an Emmy Award from the American Academy of Television Arts & Sciences, two fellowships from the National Endowment for the Arts, the Shelley Memorial Prize, the Charity Randall Citation, and a Lannan Literary Award. In 1996, she was a National Book Award Finalist for *The Terrible Stories* and was the only poet ever to have two books (*next: new poems* and *good woman: poems and a memoir 1969–1980*) chosen as finalists for the Pulitzer Prize in the same year. Appointed a Chancellor of The Academy of American Poets in 1999 and elected a Fellow in Literature of The American Academy of Arts and Sciences, Clifton currently resides in Columbia, Maryland, where she is a Distinguished Professor of Humanities at St. Mary's College.

■

BOA EDITIONS, LTD.

AMERICAN POETS CONTINUUM SERIES

Vol. 1 *The Fuhrer Bunker: A Cycle of Poems in Progress*
W. D. Snodgrass

Vol. 2 *She*
M. L. Rosenthal

Vol. 3 *Living With Distance*
Ralph J. Mills, Jr.

Vol. 4 *Not Just Any Death*
Michael Waters

Vol. 5 *That Was Then: New and Selected Poems*
Isabella Gardner

Vol. 6 *Things That Happen Where There Aren't Any People*
William Stafford

Vol. 7 *The Bridge of Change: Poems 1974–1980*
John Logan

Vol. 8 *Signatures*
Joseph Stroud

Vol. 9 *People Live Here: Selected Poems 1949–1983*
Louis Simpson

Vol. 10 *Yin*
Carolyn Kizer

Vol. 11 *Duhamel: Ideas of Order in Little Canada*
Bill Tremblay

Vol. 12 *Seeing It Was So*
Anthony Piccione

Vol. 13 *Hyam Plutzik: The Collected Poems*

Vol. 14 *Good Woman: Poems and a Memoir 1969–1980*
Lucille Clifton

Vol. 15 *Next: New Poems*
Lucille Clifton

Vol. 16 *Roxa: Voices of the Culver Family*
William B. Patrick

Vol. 17 *John Logan: The Collected Poems*

Vol. 18 *Isabella Gardner: The Collected Poems*

Vol. 19 *The Sunken Lightship*
Peter Makuck

Vol. 20 *The City in Which I Love You*
Li-Young Lee

Vol. 21 *Quilting: Poems 1987–1990*
Lucille Clifton

Vol. 22 *John Logan: The Collected Fiction*

Vol. 23 *Shenandoah and Other Verse Plays*
Delmore Schwartz

Vol. 24 *Nobody Lives on Arthur Godfrey Boulevard*
Gerald Costanzo

Vol. 25 *The Book of Names: New and Selected Poems*
Barton Sutter

Vol. 26 *Each in His Season*
W. D. Snodgrass

Vol. 27 *Wordworks: Poems Selected and New*
Richard Kostelanetz

Vol. 28 *What We Carry*
Dorianne Laux

Vol. 29 *Red Suitcase*
Naomi Shihab Nye

Vol. 30 *Song*
Brigit Pegeen Kelly

Vol. 31 *The Fuehrer Bunker: The Complete Cycle*
W. D. Snodgrass

Vol. 32 *For the Kingdom*
Anthony Piccione

Vol. 33 *The Quicken Tree*
Bill Knott

Vol. 34 *These Upraised Hands*
William B. Patrick

Vol. 35 *Crazy Horse in Stillness*
William Heyen

■

colophon

The publication of this book was made possible,
in part, by the special support of the following individuals:

Janet Aalfs, Debra Audet,
Richard Garth & Mimi Hwang
Dane & Judy Gordon, Robert & Willy Hursh,
Erica Jen, Archie & Pat Kutz, Jennifer & Craig Litt,
Boo Poulin, Deborah Ronnen,
Andrea & Paul Rubery, Pat & Michael Wilder,
and Sabra Wood.

This book was set in Optima fonts
by Richard Foerster, York Beach, Maine.
The cover was designed by Geri McCormick,
Rochester, New York.
Manufacturing by McNaughton & Gunn,
Ann Arbor, Michigan.

■